# Big Buildings

**THIS EDITION**
**Editorial Management** by Oriel Square
**Produced for DK** by WonderLab Group LLC
Jennifer Emmett, Erica Green, Kate Hale, *Founders*

**Editors** Grace Hill Smith, Libby Romero, Maya Myers, Michaela Weglinski;
**Photography Editors** Kelley Miller, Annette Kiesow, Nicole DiMella;
**Managing Editor** Rachel Houghton; **Designers** Project Design Company;
**Researcher** Michelle Harris; **Copy Editor** Lori Merritt; **Indexer** Connie Binder; **Proofreader** Larry Shea;
**Reading Specialist** Dr. Jennifer Albro; **Curriculum Specialist** Elaine Larson

Published in the United States by DK Publishing
1745 Broadway, 20th Floor, New York, NY 10019

Copyright © 2023 Dorling Kindersley Limited
DK, a Division of Penguin Random House LLC
23 24 25 26 10 9 8 7 6 5 4 3 2 1
001-334073-July/2023

All rights reserved.
Without limiting the rights under the copyright reserved above, no part of this publication may be reproduced, stored in or introduced into a retrieval system, or transmitted, in any form, or by any means (electronic, mechanical, photocopying, recording, or otherwise), without the prior written permission of the copyright owner.
Published in Great Britain by Dorling Kindersley Limited

A catalog record for this book
is available from the Library of Congress.
HC ISBN: 978-0-7440-7390-4
PB ISBN: 978-0-7440-7391-1

DK books are available at special discounts when purchased in bulk for sales promotions, premiums, fundraising, or educational use. For details, contact: DK Publishing Special Markets,
1745 Broadway, 20th Floor, New York, NY 10019
SpecialSales@dk.com

Printed and bound in China

The publisher would like to thank the following for their kind permission to reproduce their images:
a=above; c=center; b=below; l=left; r=right; t=top; b/g=background

**Dreamstime.com:** David Acosta Allely 12-13, 23cla, Bjeayes 19bc, Dan Breckwoldt 16-17, Dvrcan 3cb, Emicristea 8-9, 23tl, Europhotos 8br, F11photo 19bl, Gary718 18br, Goncharovaia 15br, Jeremyreds 10br, Pius Lee 10-11, 23clb, Lunamarina 18-19, Marcorubino 11br, Lisa Mckown 13br, Minnystock 9br, Mr.phatcharakorn Naknoon 14br, Kirill Neiezhmakov 17br, Sean Pavone 4-5, 4-5 (b/g), Matyas Rehak 21bl, Pongpon Rinthaisong 1b, Mabelin Santos 13bc, Anthony Aneese Totah Jr 17bc, Sharlotta Ulrikh 22, Vitalyedush 21bc, Shao-chun Wang 6-7, 23bl, Jinfeng Zhang / Laozhang 16br; **Getty Images / iStock:** Eloi_Omella 6br, simonbradfield 20-21, 23cl, SL_Photography 14-15; **Shutterstock.com:** Iurii Buriak 15bl, Fortgens Photography 12br, Martin Mecnarowski 4cb, Kevin Ruck 11bl

Cover images: *Back:* **Dreamstime.com:** Vectomart (cra, clb)

All other images © Dorling Kindersley
For more information see: www.dkimages.com

**For the curious**
**www.dk.com**

# Big Buildings

Libby Romero

There are lots of big buildings around the world. Let us visit them!

This very tall building is a skyscraper.

**skyscraper**
[SKY-skray-per]

Some rulers lived in castles.

**castles**
[KA-sulls]

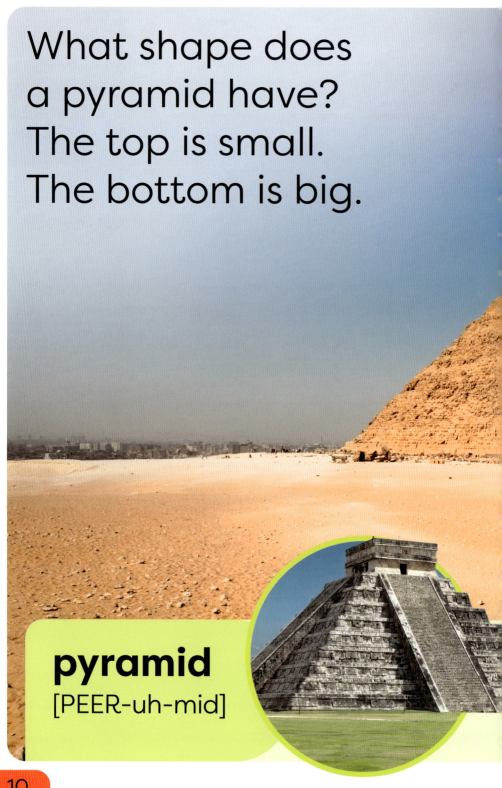

What shape does a pyramid have? The top is small. The bottom is big.

**pyramid**
[PEER-uh-mid]

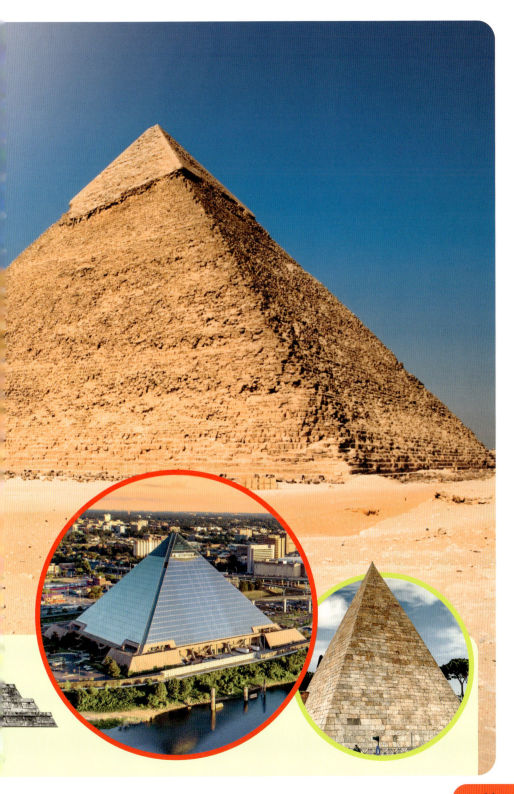

Some museums have lots of colors. Which colors can you see?

**museums**
[mew-ZEE-ums]

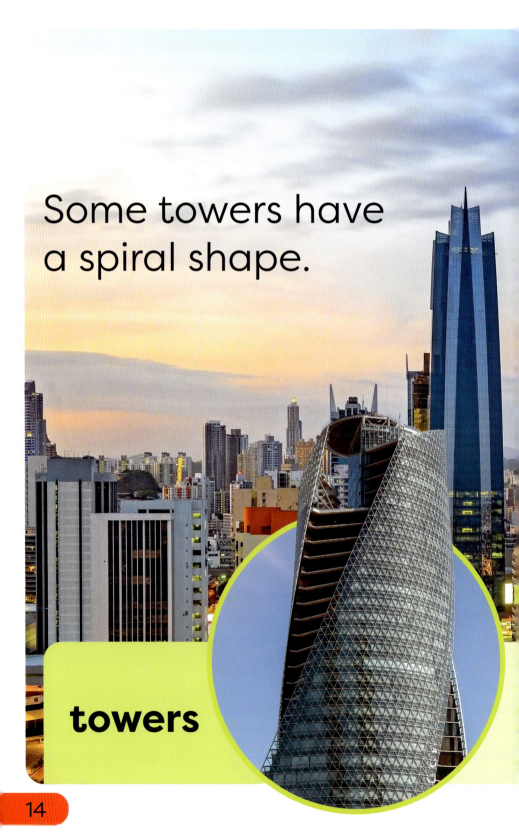

Some towers have a spiral shape.

**towers**

Some buildings are round, like a ball.

**round**

17

Look at the big clock tower.
What time is it?

**clock tower**

An opera house is where people sing. This one looks like a sailboat!

**opera house**

Look up!
Look around!
See all the
big buildings.

# Glossary

**castle**
a strong building that can protect people living inside

**museum**
a place that displays things like art, science, and historical items

**opera house**
a theater where people perform music and shows

**pyramid**
a building with a square base and triangular sides that meet in a point

**skyscraper**
a very tall building

# Quiz

Answer the questions to see what you've learned. Check your answers with an adult.

1. What is a skyscraper?
2. Where did some rulers live?
3. Is a pyramid bigger at the bottom or the top?
4. What does a clock tower tell you?
5. If you could build a big building, what would it look like?

1. A very tall building  2. In castles  3. The bottom
4. What time it is  5. Answers will vary